BEING A TEENAGER ROCKS

BEING A TEENAGER

ROCKS

AN INTRODUCTION TO THE WORLD OF THE 21ST CENTURY TEENAGER
Vol 1

GILLIAN DALLAS

THIS BOOK BELONGS TO:

- -

Being a Teenager Rocks: An Introduction to the world of the 21st Century Teenager
Original Edition published by SkoolKnews Publishing House
No portion of this book may be reproduced, stored in a retrieval system, or transmitted in any form or by any means, except for brief quotations in printed reviews without prior written permission of Skoolknews or Gillian Dallas.
Published by
SKnews
Copyright©2023 SkoolKnews Publishing House
ISBN: 978-1-64775-5829
Author: Gillian Dallas
Illustrations: Howard Lindsay
Layout Artists: Judith Taylor, Maurice Palmer, and Gillian Dallas

CONTENTS

ACKNOWLEDGEMENT IV

PREFACE V

CHARACTERISTICS OF A TEENAGER 1

STAGES OF DEVELOPMENT DURING ADOLESCENCE 7

CHANGING TRENDS AMONG THE TEENAGERS OF THE 20TH CENTURY VERSUS THE 21ST CENTURY 11

THINGS I SHOULD AVOID DOING AS A TEEN 18

FEARS I FACE AS A TEENAGER 23

THINGS THAT MAKE ME HAPPY AS A TEENAGER 24

CHALLENGES FACED BY THE 21ST CENTURY TEENAGER 26

TIPS TEENAGERS CAN APPLY WHEN FACED WITH DIFFICULT CHALLENGES 30

REPLACING NEGATIVE WORDS WITH POSITIVE ONES 33

POPULAR TEENAGE VOCABULARY (SLANGS AND SLURS) 36

FUTURE DREAMS AND CAREERS 38

HEALTHY HABITS FOR AN EFFECTIVE TEENAGER 43

AFFIRMATIONS I CAN APPLY AS A TEENAGER TO GUIDE ME ON THE PATH TO SUCCESS 57

ACKNOWLEDGEMENT

I would love to express special thanks to all the teenagers as well as friends who helped me in the creation of this book.

PREFACE

Being a teenager opens a new world to endless possibilities. A world filled with excitement as well as challenges. So many lifestyle changes that occur in this period allow a new identity to be formed.

As a teenager, at times, you feel as if you are misunderstood by your parents or the adults in your environment. The many changes in your body and emotions cause you to ask questions, some of which are left unanswered. Subsequently, you begin to explore, query, and investigate ways to create solutions that allow you to cope. These solutions are not always suitable; hence challenges and conflicts arise. However, it is a period where mistakes are made, and lessons are learnt.

There are many decisions you will make, and these may be difficult at times as the outcomes are variable. Hence, being actively engaged in positive and motivational exercises will allow you to have an easier transition into young adulthood.

Gillian Dallas

CHARACTERISTICS OF A TEENAGER

WHAT MAKES ME A TEENAGER?

- Age - A person in age ranging from 13 to 19 years
- Puberty
- Growth spurt
- Production of hormones

Testosterone for males:

- Causing deep voice
- Broadening of the chest
- Facial hair
- Hair on pubic regions

Progesterone and Estrogen **for females:**

- Release of egg
- Monthly cycle (menstruation)
- Broadening of the hips and narrowing of the waist, enlargement of the breast
- Self-awareness: becoming more aware of your feelings and personality

Change in Emotions

- **Frequent changes in emotions** - for example, happy at this moment then sad for no reason
- **Uncertainties and Indecisiveness** – decisions are not easy to make as you are not sure if the decision made will bring a positive outcome
- **Peer Pressure** – pressure from peers and friends to do things that will allow you to be accepted by the group

Getting to explore new things and their environment without the assistance of parents for example:
- Shopping
- Going to the barber and hairdresser
- Going to school and church

Figuring out how to do things on your own for example, domestic chores such as:
- Cooking a meal, washing, and ironing clothes, sewing, and hemming clothes
- Feeding and taking care of pets or younger siblings
- Reading a manual and setting up a device

Grooming

- Being more interested in your appearance such as having new hairstyles, and new clothes

Attraction and Development of Sexual feelings for others

- Associated with reaching sexual maturity

What are the signs that indicate physical development for the adolescent male?

___

What are the signs that indicate physical development for the adolescent female?

___

What is the significance of independence in the developmental process of adolescence?

_____

_____

_____

_____

_____

Explain the importance of grooming in the life of a teenager.

_____

_____

_____

_____

_____

_____

_____

_____

_____

_____

_____

STAGES OF DEVELOPMENT DURING ADOLESCENCE

Stage	Age	Physical Development	Cognitive Development	Psychosocial Development	Sexual Maturity and Intimacy
Early Adolescence	10 - 14	Growth spurt begins. Development of secondary sexual characteristics	Develops more intellectual interest, concrete, and critical thinking skills, less interest in abstract thinking and future goals	Awareness heightens about self and body image/Mood swings. The desire for independence increases	Increase awareness in sexuality and sexual orientation. Making stronger commitments among peer group/Formation of strong friendships
Middle Adolescence	15 - 16	Physical growth continues for boys while girls' growth, begin to slow down	Focus more on future goals, capacity increases for abstract and critical thinking	Exploration of self-identity and lifestyles changes. For example: Body piercing, Tattooing, Body building, Dieting, Grooming. Strong peer influence that can contribute to Risky behaviours such as: substance abuse- alcohol, cocaine, crack, heroin, molly pills, tobacco, marijuana, marijuana edibles -cookies, cakes, vaping transactional sex vandalism gang involvement	Exposure to sexual acts and sexually explicit materials. Sexting, Experimentations with different forms of sexual expressions, for example, masturbation. Increase interest in sexual relationships
Late Adolescence	17 - 19		More advanced abstract and rational thinking and decision making. More goal oriented and futuristic thinking	A more stable sense of identity and autonomy	Formation of committed relationships

List at least three cognitive changes that occur during adolescence.

_____
_____
_____
_____
_____
_____
_____

Give examples of some lifestyle changes that you have incorporated since the onset of puberty.

_____
_____
_____
_____
_____
_____
_____
_____
_____
_____

Why are your friends important to you? State at least three reasons.

_____
_____
_____
_____
_____
_____
_____
_____

Peers play an important role in the life of a teen. Identify some of the positive ways your peers have influenced you.

_____
_____
_____
_____
_____
_____
_____
_____

Identify some of the negative ways your peers have influenced you.

CHANGING TRENDS AMONG THE TEENAGERS OF THE 20TH CENTURY VERSUS THE 21ST CENTURY

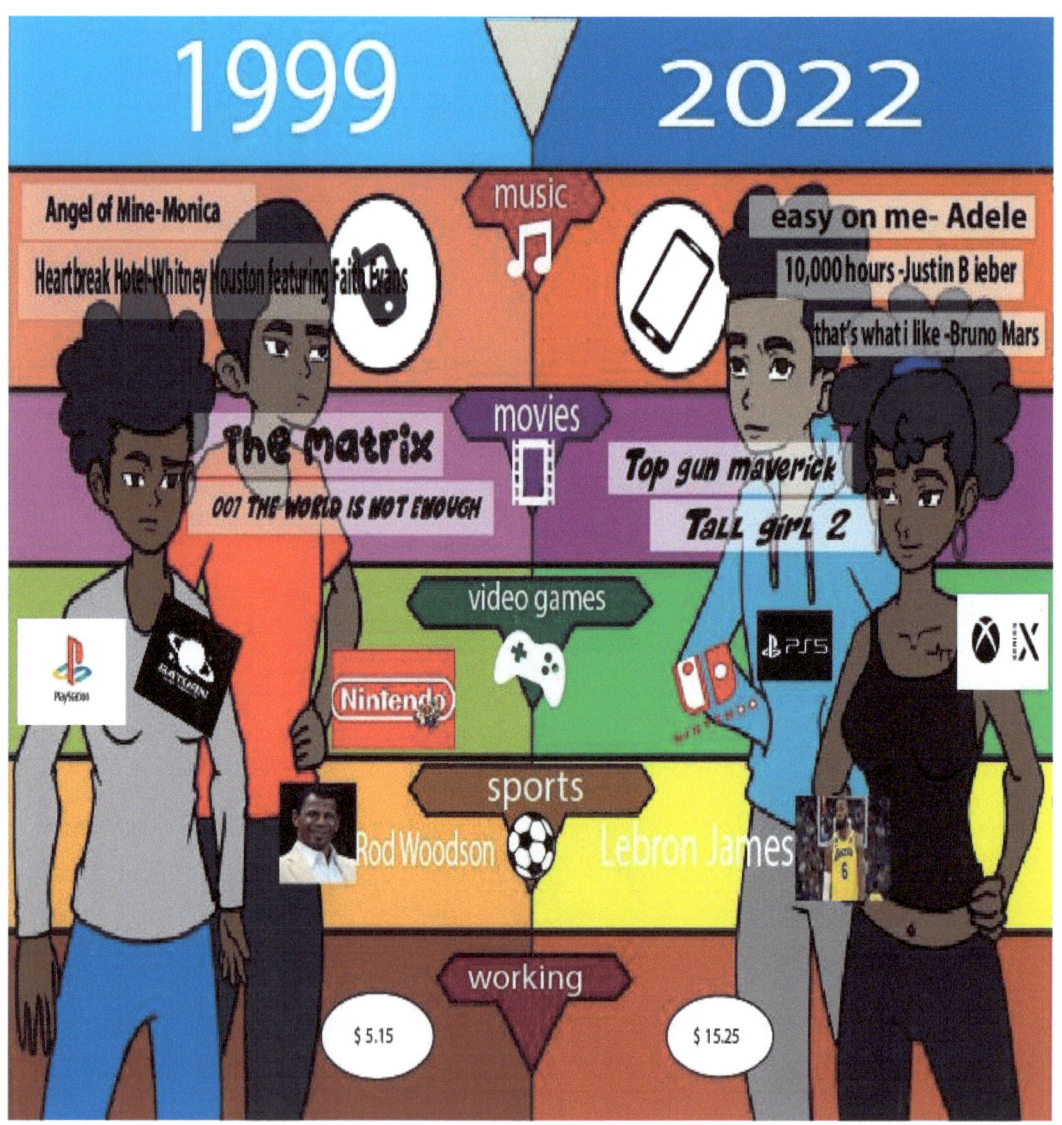

20th Century Teenage Boys	20th Century Teenage Girls	21st Century Teenage Boys	21st Century Teenage Girls
Primary, Secondary and Tertiary School Education: Vocational training programmes - building, auto-mechanics, electrical, technical drawing, art and craft, carpentry, plumbing, agriculture, horticulture, landscaping	Primary and Secondary School Education: Skills training programmes - home management, home economics, clothing, and textiles, cosmetology and art and craft. **Note:** Girls were seen as the primary caregiver so they would need these skills to run an efficient home and take care of their husbands and children	Primary and Secondary School Education: Skills programmes - building, auto mechanics, electrical, technical drawing, design arts, welding, mechanical engineering, construction management, chef, phlebotomy, dental assistant, dental hygienists, radiology, barbering, hairstyling, veterinary assistant, web design, marketing, communication, and design, pipe-fitting, machining, plumbing, carpentry	Primary and Secondary School Education: Skills programmes - home management, cosmetology, art and craft, nursing assistant, medical coding, massage therapy, cooking, data and programming, education, web design and training, marketing, communication and design, Veterinary assistant, sonography, phlebotomy, construction management, dental hygienists, plumbing, carpentry
Sports: Football, Rugby, Cricket, Track and Field, Basketball, Volleyball, Lacrosse Hockey, Lacrosse, Boxing, Kickboxing, Wrestling, Diving. **Note:** Boys were seen as, the Primary Home Earner, so they were expected to be strong and were likely to keep up with these aggressive sports and programmes	**Sports:** Netball, Track and Field, Volleyball, Swimming, Gymnastics, Hockey, Ice-Hockey, Baseball, Basketball, Cricket.	**Sports:** Football, Rugby, Hockey, Ice-hockey, Baseball, Cricket, Track and Field, Basketball, Volleyball, Lacrosse, Boxing, Kickboxing, Wrestling. **Note:** Sports programmes are no longer gender specific in the 21st Century both boys and girls are accepted to play any type of sports	**Sports:** Netball, Track and Field, Volleyball, Lacrosse, Swimming, Gymnastics, Wrestling, Cricket, Basketball, Baseball, Boxing. **Note:** However, most games when they are being played the members of the team are of the same sex, this means that males and female do not participate on the same team.

20th Century Teenage Boys	20th Century Teenage Girls	21st Century Teenage Boys	21st Century Teenage Girls
Domestic Care: sweeping yard, cutting the lawn, washing windows and doors, washing motor vehicles, painting, carrying out garbage, vacuuming cars, and upholsters, cleaning up litter, grooming pets, feeding pets, cleaning and washing animal pens if parents raise livestock, pruning trees **Note:** Chores were gender assigned. Certain chores were assumed too masculine for females to do	**Domestic Care:** sweeping and wiping the floors, cleaning of bedrooms and bathrooms, washing the dishes and laundry, sewing and mending of clothes, or household apparel, doing laundry, folding and putting away clothes, cooking and baking, babysitting younger siblings, preparing and cooking meals, setting, and clearing table **Note:** Chores were gender assigned. Certain chores were assumed too feminine for males carry out	**Domestic Care:** Sweeping yard, Cutting the lawn, Washing motor vehicles, painting, carrying out garbage, mending clothes, doing laundry, babysitting younger siblings, vacuuming cars and upholsters, cleaning up litter, grooming pets, feeding pets, pruning trees, washing dishes, setting and clearing tables, preparing and cooking of meals	**Domestic Care:** Babysitting younger siblings, doing laundry, mending clothes and preparing and cooking meals, vacuuming furniture, sweeping and wiping floors, cleaning bedrooms and bathrooms, washing dishes, painting, carrying out garbage, cleaning up litter, grooming pets, feeding pets, pruning shrubs, and watering plants. **Note:** In most homes in the 21st century chores are not gender assigned. The male or female teenager is assigned the role based on what needs to be done within the home.

20th Century Teenage Boys	20th Century Teenage Girls	21st Century Teenage Boys	21st Century Teenage Girls
Leisure Time: going to the football field to play ball, riding your bicycle through the community or housing scheme, running tires and wheels, making cotton wheels carts and box carts, playing cricket, playing marbles, playing dominoes and ludo, playing snake and ladder, playing scrabble and card games, playing gigs and yoyo, heisting kites and making catapults (slingshots), making bows and arrows, making fish guns, making snares, going bird hunting, making paper boats and planes, listening to music from loud boom boxing playing, going to dance and parties unchaperoned, going to picnic and cookouts and church trips	**Leisure Time:** reading a novel, singing, or dancing, playing ring games, playing jacks, playing hopscotch, skipping, playing dandy shandy (sighting), talking on the phone, playing cards games, playing ludo, playing monopoly, playing snakes and ladder, playing scrabble, playing Pictionary, texting, sending emails, watching movies, attending sleepovers, going to the movies, going parties chaperoned, going to picnic and cookout and church trips.	**Leisure Time:** playing sports mainly football, cricket, basketball and volleyball, jogging, exercising mainly strength training and weight-lifting, dodge ball, spud, paintball, playing video games with gaming systems such as Nintendo, Xbox, play station, PS5, playing digital games, driving go-cart, watching television, listening to music, create and practice new dance moves, blogging, creating videos on Facebook, Tik Tok and Instagram playing of board games, texting, making phone calls, going to parties, hanging out at the mall, going to the movies with friends, going on camping and church trips, surfing and diving	**Leisure Time:** talking on the phone with friends, using apps such as Facebook, Tik Tok and Instagram, watching television, playing games on phone or tablets, texting, emailing, reading novels online, blogging, watching movies, dancing to music, learning new dance moves, shopping and going to the mall with friends, partying, going to the spa, dining, playing board of games, going to the beach, going camping and cookouts and barbeques, going on church and family trips

20th Century Teenage Boys	20th Century Teenage Girls	21st Century Teenage Boys	21st Century Teenage Girls
Expected Social Behaviour: confident, projected, and deep voice, physically strong, agile, charismatic, unsentimental, calm, respectful	**Expected Social Behaviour:** emotional and caring, compassionate, polite, sentimental, effervescent, soft-spoken	**Expected Social Behaviour:** Males are expected to be more emotional, expressive, confident, charismatic, caring, respectful	**Expected Social Behaviour:** Females are expected to be gentle, caring, compassionate, expressive, polite, respectful
Expected Dress: Formal Attire Shirts must be tucked inside the pants, while belts worn must be buckled. Pants should be long enough to cover socks. Socks must be worn with shoes. Hair must be cut unless you are a Rastafarian (Rastas do not cut hair) and properly groomed. Shoes must be polished. A tie must be worn with formal attire. Socks should not be seen if the male is wearing a pant.	**Expected Dress: Formal Attire** Blouses must be tucked in skirts or pants. Stockings must be worn with shoes. Belts must be worn if there are loops in the garment. Skirts must be worn at the hemline or below the knees. Hair must be combed or properly groomed.	**Expected Dress: Formal Attire** Shirts can be worn inside or out. Pants can be worn three-quarter length or ankle length. Shirts can be worn without a tie. Belts are optional. Shoes can be worn without socks. Hair is expected to be styled or properly groomed.	**Expected Dress: Formal Attire –** Blouses must be tucked in skirts or pants or worn outside. Stockings are optional with shoes. Belts are optional when wearing a garment. Skirts worn can be of a variety of lengths: at the hemline, below the knees, ankle length, mini, etc. Hair is expected to be styled or properly groomed.

20th Century Teenage Boys	20th Century Teenage Girls	21st Century Teenage Boys	21st Century Teenage Girls
Expected Dress: Casual Attire Shirts can be tucked inside the pants or worn outside for example, a T-shirt or sports shirt. Belts must be buckled. Underwear should not be seen. Clothes can be close fitted but not skin-tight.	Expected Dress: Casual Attire Shirt can be tucked inside the pants or worn outside for example, a T-shirt or sports shirt. Belt must be buckled. Underwear should not be seen. Clothes can be close fitted but not skin-tight. The attire worn should not expose breasts and buttocks and pubic regions.	Expected Dress: Casual Attire Shirt can be tucked inside the pants or worn outside for example, a T-shirt or sports shirt. Belts are optional when wearing pants or shorts. Underwear should not be seen. Clothes can be close fitted or skin -tight.	Expected Dress: Casual Attire Shirt can be tucked inside the pants or worn outside for example, a T-shirt or sports shirt. Belt must be buckled. Underwear should not be seen. Clothes can be close fitted or skin-tight. The attire should not expose the nipples and buttocks and pubic regions.

Write a blog or an email to a 20th century teenager explaining why you think your leisure time is more entertaining than theirs. What are the areas you would outline? Give reasons for your choices.

THINGS I SHOULD AVOID DOING AS A TEEN

1. Using social media and the Internet inappropriately:

- Posting nude pictures and videos
- Watching pornographic videos
- Posting brawls and vulgar behaviour
- Sending lewd texts
- Cyberbullying
- Posting fake news
- Talking and giving out personal information to persons you do not know

2. Drinking alcoholic beverages such as:
- Rum
- Beer
- Alcoholic wine
- Champagne

3. Smoking and doing Illicit Drugs
- Marijuana
- Crack
- Heroin
- Cocaine
- Tobacco
- Cigarette
- Vaping

4. **Gambling**
    - Lotto
    - Cash pot
    - Pick 3
    - Pick 4
    - Scratchers

5. **Stealing**
6. **Scamming**

7. **Violence:**
    - Gangs
    - Brawls
    - Fights
    - Use of deadly weapons

8. Sexual Indulgence:
- Petting
- Kissing
- Sex
- Having multiple sexual partners

9. Disobedience:
- Speaking disrespectfully to parents and others
- Telling lies to parents
- Reluctant to carry out duties

Identify some behaviours to avoid as a teen.

___

Create a poem or song addressing some of these negative behaviours that teens must avoid.

___

FEARS I FACE AS A TEENAGER

- Disappointing parents
- Rejection/Abandonment
- Peer Pressure
- Dying/ Losing parents/Not being remembered
- Teenage Pregnancy
- Failure to succeed
- Discrimination
- Anger and Abuse from parents and peers
- Poverty
- Rape
- Abduction

THINGS THAT MAKE ME HAPPY AS A TEENAGER

- ♥ Affection from peers and family
- ♥ Praise from family members especially parent(s)
- ♥ Maintaining a good relationship with parent(s)
- ♥ Academic success
- ♥ Mastery of various tasks

Doing certain activities such as:
- ♥ Riding a bicycle and playing video games
- ♥ Playing sports
- ♥ Watching TV or reading a book ♥
- Talking to friends/FaceTime
- ♥ Partying
- ♥ Shopping and dining
- ♥ Keeping healthy – sleep, recreation

- ♥ Respecting boundaries - Parents and family members acknowledging my space
- ♥ Getting gifts and having some level of financial Independence
- ♥ Positive public recognition- getting awards and approval, social approval, and being popular

Create a digital/manual portfolio of the things that make you happy as a teen. You can share it with your parents, family, and friends.

CHALLENGES FACED BY THE 21ST CENTURY TEENAGER

- Anxiety
- Depression- Suicidal thoughts
- Self-loathing
- Body shaming
- Identity crisis
- Self-worth
- Low self-esteem
- Verbal Abuse
- Drug Abuse
- Alcohol Abuse
- Sexual Abuse
- Stress and frustration from low-socio-economic background
- Peer pressure

- Bullying
- Cyberbullying
- Gang violence

- Loss of family member(s)
- Eating disorders
- Promiscuity
- Poor academic performance
- Social Anxiety
- Relationships- Parental conflicts /Intimate relationship

Create a script for a reel video advising teenagers on how to address a particular issue affecting them, for example, suicidal thoughts, gang violence, depression, drug/sexual abuse, or any other challenging issue.

List at least three groups or agencies that can offer counselling or advice to struggling teenagers.

TIPS TEENAGERS CAN APPLY WHEN FACED WITH DIFFICULT CHALLENGES

1. Speak to someone who you think is trustworthy, for example, a guidance counsellor, teacher, pastor, or principal.
2. Express yourself using different methods such as:
   - Journaling - have a notebook or diary
   - Blogging - use a cell phone or other devices to create positive blogs, podcasts, and videos instead of negative ones. (Share responsibly)
   - Writing positive poetry and songs
   - Create new dance moves
3. Finding an environment that brings a calming effect:
   - Going to the beach
   - Nature walk /Rock climbing

- Listening to music
- White noise
- Meditating

- Worshipping
- Swimming
- Exercise
- Dancing
- Star gazing
- Silence

- Speak to an expert who is knowledgeable about the situation you face
- Do not take yourself too seriously; laugh sometimes at yourself
- Identifying the specific challenges, you need to overcome is one of the first steps to getting the solution

REPLACING NEGATIVE WORDS WITH POSITIVE ONES

WORDS I MUST AVOID 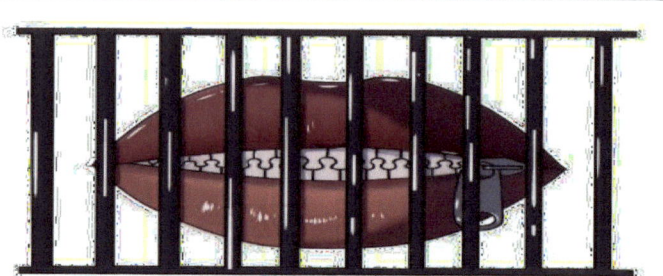	I SHOULD REPLACE THE NEGATIVE WORDS WITH POSITIVE ONES 
I cannot be bothered.	I must try again.
I give up it is just too hard.	Giving up is not one of my options.
I am tired of this.	I will rest and try again.
I just want this to end.	This will end when I succeed.
I want to die.	I will push harder to achieve my end goal.
What is the point of doing this? I will still fail.	Most success comes from failed attempts.
I am a failure.	It's okay to have flaws and imperfections as making mistakes is part of being a human.
I am a loser.	Success is most empowering after failure.
Makes no sense trying because it is a lost cause.	Trials and errors result in success.

I am a dunce.	I am ignorant in that area so I will be patient until I have become knowledgeable in that subject area.
I can never do anything right.	Everyone makes mistakes; that is how he or she knows how to improve or correct the wrong.
Might as well give up because no matter how hard I try I am not successful.	Success is not merited by others but by how I perceive it to be.

Create a motivational speech demonstrating the use of positive words to overcome challenging situations.

POPULAR TEENAGE VOCABULARY
(SLANGS AND SLURS)

- **Male Friend:** Dawg, Chargie, Bredda, Choppa, Bro, Crocs, Gad, buddy, Mate, Chum, Amigo, Dude, Champ, Junior, Shortie, Punk
- **Female Friend:** Gurl, Bebe, Doll, Dollie, Barbie, Sistah, Sistah Gal, Gal, Girly, Queen, BFF, Bestie, Best Fran, Missy, Chica
- **Persons held in high respect:** Godfather, Mi G, Elder, Bro God, My Lord, Uncle, Coach, Mumma, Auntie
- **Throw/Cuss Words:** Waste Man, Waste gal, Yam head, Yamballa, Idiot, Gal Clown, Weirdo, Loudmouth
- **Body Appearance:** Body Good, Body Clean, Mumma heavy, Slimaz, Slim-thick, Thickaz, Curvy, Fluffy, Diva, Browning

TEXT TERMINOLOGY

Omg- Oh my God, dwl- dying with laughter, lol- laugh out loud, rofl- roll on the floor and laugh, wassup- what's up, ihu- I hear you, Irk- I know right, Idc- I don't care, nvm- never mind, wym- what do you mean, wyd-what you are doing, lmao- laugh my ass off, hru- how are you, thx- thanks, sml- smile, Idk- I do not know, tlc- tender loving care, lel- laugh extra loud, brb- be right back,

sus- suspicious, dope- cool, ty-thank you, sic- cool, ttyl- talk to you later, fyi- for your information, txt- text, wlx- welcome, btw- by the way, asap- as soon as possible, g2g- got to go, b4n- bye for now, smh- shake my head, okl- okay cool, frl- for real, omw- on my way, b4- before, hbu- how about you, str8- straight, Idm- I do not mind, llu- I love you, wpn- what happened, rip- rest in peace, yolo- hello, hun/hon- honey, gm- good morning, gn- good night, ppl- people

FUTURE DREAMS AND CAREERS

To be successful in:
- Getting a higher education
- Business
- Joining the Armed/ Security Forces
- Homeowner / Real Estate
- Parenting

To become a professional in the field of Science, Arts, Sports, and Business for example:
- Software Developers Application
- Software Developers, Systems Software
- Professional Traveler
- Sustainable Development Planner

- Wedding Planner/Party Planner
- Personal Shopper
- Financial Adviser / Financial Coach
- Professional Athlete
- Civil Engineer
- Computer Engineer
- Computer Systems Analyst
- Computer Support Specialist
- Medical Scientist
- Animator
- Astronaut
- Social Media Influencer
- Life Coach
- Dentist / Dental Hygienist
- Personal Trainer
- Certified Ethical Hacker
- Professional Blogger
- Marketing Research Analyst
- Marketing Manager
- Fiber Optic Technician
- Robot Technician
- Space Mechanic

- Physician /Surgeon/ Physician Assistant/ Registered Nurse
- Physical Therapist/ Mental health therapist
- Physiologist
- Radiologist/ Radiographer
- Judges/ Lawyers/ Clerk of the Courts
- Retirement Counsellor
- Information security analyst
- Accountant/Auditors
- Project Manager
- General and operation Manager
- Financial Managers
- Leisure Consultant
- Real Estate Agents
- Logistics Coordinator
- Inventory/Logistics Manager

- Logistics Officer
- Shipping Manager
- Senior Engineering Specialist
- Sous Chef
- Dietitian
- Comedian
- Restaurant manager
- Executive chef
- Culinary manager
- Food service manager
- Private Chef
- Disc Jockey/Music Producer/Dancer
- Social Media Manager /Journalist
- Entrepreneur
- Fashion retailer/Model/Graphic Designer
- Farmer

Create a vision board of your dreams, goals, and inspirations.

HEALTHY HABITS FOR AN EFFECTIVE TEENAGER

1. Planning - Planning will allow me to set appropriate goals. Consistent planning will help me to prioritize which goals are realistic and most achievable.
2. Planning will allow me to be efficient in the tasks or projects I execute. Hence, I may use fewer resources and time and save money.
3. Planning will help me to be prepared for emergencies that may occur during events or tasks or projects.
4. Planning will let me become a good organizer, where I am proactive, planning instead of being reactive and waiting until something happens.

Maintaining a good routine- lessens anxiety and stress, promotesa healthy immune system, and promotes healthy mental and emotional well-being. Examples of good routines:

- Good sleeping habits- I must ensure that I have at least 8- 10 hours of sleep. I must avoid too much screen time at night as this will reduce my sleeping hours and prevent me from engaging effectively in my daytime activities.
- Good eating habits- I must ensure that I have breakfast, as this is the first meal of the day. Eating whole grains, proteins, and fruits in the morning will keep me energized. I must also eat balanced meals so I will get the right proportion of each nutrient in my diet. Eat fruits and

vegetables daily, not eating sweets such as lollipops and drinking sodas are also ways that I can maintain a healthy lifestyle.

- Maintaining good personal hygiene by investing in self-care. I must ensure that I will take a bath once per day. I must brush my teeth at least three times per day or rinse my mouth and floss after each meal. I must change my clothes each day and after engaging in activities that make me perspire. I must ensure that my attire is socially

  accepted. For example, my pants should not be exposing my buttocks, whether I am a male or female. Also, if I am a female, I must ensure that my blouse is not too tight so that my breasts are not exposed.

- I must maintain a good exercise routine where I will try to carry out daily exercises such as jogging, walking, boxing, aerobic training, skipping, strength training, exercise, dancing, and squatting. Daily exercise will promote a healthy immune system and help my body to release

  endorphins that will allow me to relax reducing tension and anxieties.

Create a weekly calendar outlining a routine that promotes a healthy teenage life. This should include:

- Time slots
- Personal hygiene
- Schoolwork/School activities
- Leisure/social activities
- Mental development
- Chores
- Other activities

_____
_____
_____
_____
_____
_____
_____
_____
_____

Maintaining a clean environment:

- I must ensure that my environment is clean, tidy, and free from clutter.
- I must ensure that my kitchen sink is clear of dirty dishes to keep away pests and vectors such as rats and flies.
- I must ensure that my books, clothes, and shoes are placed in the designated areas so as not to cause harm or accidents.
- I must ensure that my dirty clothes are placed in the clothes or laundry bins so my room or the rooms that I share with others do not become smelly and unpleasant because of not maintaining proper domestic care.

- I must ensure that I do not eat in my bedroom or if I do eat in my room, I clean up afterward to avoid unpleasant odours, pests, and vectors that may cause illnesses.
- I must ensure that I clean up spills off the table or floors immediately.
- I must ensure that I throw away garbage daily from inside the home to avoid creating housefly breeding grounds and other pests and vectors such as rats and cockroaches.
- Conserving Limited Resources - Conserving limited resources save money and energy.

Ways I can conserve resources in my home are:

Hot or cold shower?

- I can take short showers instead of baths.
- I must turn off the faucet when brushing my teeth, when soaping up during a bath or when washing dishes.
- I must turn off the lights when I am not using them.
- I must turn off devices when they are not in use.
- I must use water that is left over that is not full of detergent or chemicals to wash cars or to water plants.
- I must recycle paper and plastic.
- I must use as much sunlight as possible for example,

  instead of turning on a light in a room during the day to read or use my phone or tablet I can find a cool shady area outside where can still have access to the Wi-Fi.
- I must think carefully about what I may need in the freezer or refrigerator before going in to limit the frequent visits.

Create a social media challenge to promote a clean environment and or the conservation of limited resources.

Become an active listener -

- I will ensure that I listen keenly to what others are saying so I do not form opinions or judgements without understanding what is being said. I will try to ask for clarification if I do not understand what is being said to me. I will ensure to listen keenly before I make a comment or complaint or carry out an action regarding what is being said to me.

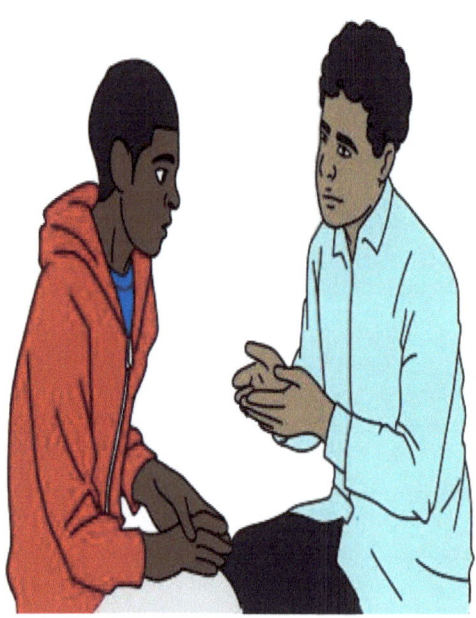

Write three statements that demonstrate that you are an active listener.

Create positive social relationships - I will ensure that I build friendships.

In addition, I will invest some of my time in others by:
- Finding others that share similar interests, hobbies, games, food, etc.
- Engage in mentorship or leadership groups such as churches, youth clubs, non-government organizations, government organizations, sports clubs, etc.
- Be a positive blogger or social media influencer
- Be a spokesperson for various charities
- Show empathy towards others

- Accept the difference in others; not everyone will share my interests and opinions, but that does not mean they cannot be in my circle. Their differences can help to give me insights when I am planning or making critical decisions.

- Build mutual trust and respect.
- Show appreciation in words and or deeds

What social group(s) are you a part of?

_____
_____
_____
_____
_____
_____
_____
_____

Describe how being a part of a social group helps you to build relationships.

_____
_____
_____
_____
_____
_____
_____
_____

In what other area(s) would you like to serve?

AFFIRMATIONS I CAN APPLY AS A TEENAGER TO GUIDE ME ON THE PATH TO SUCCESS

1. **"I am Bold: Bold as a lion and fierce as a tiger":**
- Today I choose to be bold to celebrate life, despite its challenges.

- I choose to be bold in speech, dress, dance, laughter, deeds, and spirit.
- I will be bold as a lion never accepting defeat and fierce as a tiger chasing away low self-esteem, insecurities, and doubts.

State five ways in which you have been bold.

2. I am Wise:

- I will be perceptive as the owl, that even in the dark I will be able to see light.
- I will shun the things that will inhibit my growth and dull my lustre in this present world.

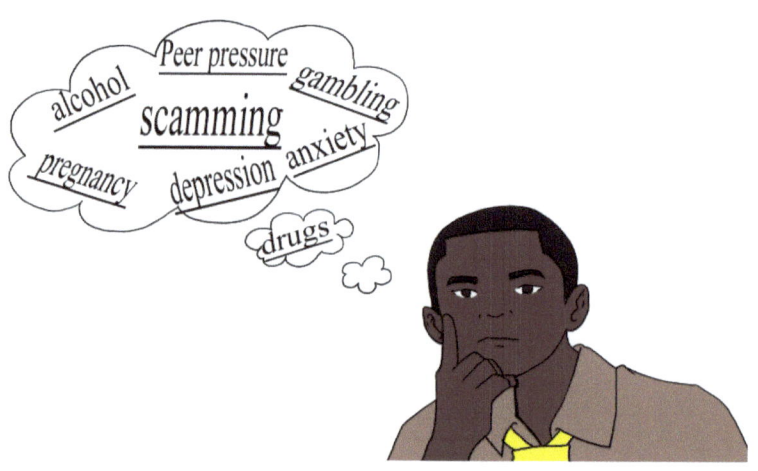

Therefore, I choose to be wise in my choices of:
- Friends
- Recreational activities
- Partnership
- Deeds
- Acts

Identify five ways you are wise as a teenager.

3. I am Strong:

I must strive to have the strength to push through negative criticisms, self, and body loathing. For me to maintain a strong character and become a leader among my peers, I must engage in:

- ✓ Exercise, meditation, extracurricular activities
- ✓ Attend Sabbath and Sunday schools
- ✓ Practice selfless acts
- ✓ Attend social events that are deemed appropriate for my age

Identify five ways that you have displayed your strengths.

4. I am a Team Member:

I am a member of a team whether it be school, home, or church. Therefore, my actions cannot always be solo as there are days I will need to strongly rely on my team and my team on me.

In order for me to be an effective team member I must ensure that I am:

- Thoughtful
- Efficient in carrying out my tasks
- Assist others who need my help
- Manage my time and affairs and that of my team wisely

State five things that you have applied in your social group or school group that will allow you to become an excellent team leader.

5. I am an Achiever:

- ✓ I will try to achieve mastery in my tasks and skills that I need even if I fail at several attempts.
- ✓ I will not give up even when I am told to do so. However, I will try to work even harder.
- ✓ I will focus on my goals and targets as the cheetah focus on her prey. Therefore, I will use my time efficiently so that in the end I will be successful in my endeavours.

Identify five things that you have achieved since the onset of puberty.

6. I am Proactive:

- ✓ I am prepared for challenges by addressing issues before they become conflicts.
- ✓ I am thoughtful, kind, and compassionate. Hence, I will speak positive words to those in my environment, such as my friends and peers so if conflicts arise, they will be easily addressed.
- ✓ I am positioning myself for positive outcomes by taking preventive measures for example:
    - Reading ahead so that I am actively engaged in my lessons
    - Developing good study habits so that I am prepared for my assessments.

Identify five ways you are proactive in your home, school, or community or church.

7. I will become a visionary leader and will invite others to share their visions:

- ✓ I am creative; I will try to find new and imaginative ways to solve problems.
- ✓ I am goal-oriented, as I will try to set time-based targets that will help me to be successful in achieving my goals.
- ✓ I am a team player and an agent of change:

I will share my visions and dreams with others and invite others to share my visions. Therefore, I will participate in extracurricular activities that will allow me to display my talents and my dreams.

- ✓ I am organized. I must ensure that I follow plans that I have created to achieve academic and social success for example:
  - Eat a healthy breakfast so that I can focus on my lessons
  - Complete my assignments on time
  - Attire properly for school
  - Have my tools such as pens, pencils, textbooks, notebooks, etc. to do my tasks effectively.
  - Help and coordinate class events.

All organizational skills that I will apply now will help me in the future to ensure that my visions will be successful.

Create an acronym for the word VISIONARY LEADER that best defines you.

8. **I am Thankful: I am thankful to the people in my environment.**

Thankful is being grateful or appreciative.
- ✓ I am thankful for my parents /caregivers, friends, family, teachers, pastors, etc., for giving care to me or facilitating aid when it was impossible to do it on my own.

- ✓ I am thankful for all the teachers that I have had relevant experiences with and those that are yet to come. Whether they are professionals or those that are teachers that teach the hid- den curriculum of life.
- ✓ I am thankful for those individuals who will stay up with me when I have nightmares to help soothe me and calm my fears.
- ✓ I am thankful for those that will say 'keep focus' when I get distracted with sorrow, anxiety, depression, pain, parties/dances, love affairs, and romance.
- ✓ I am thankful for those who will value my efforts and see my determination to succeed despite challenges.
- ✓ I am thankful for those persons who will share their comments and criticisms of my behaviour or attitudes towards work whether it is good or bad, as this will help to form the person I choose to become.
- ✓ I am thankful to the people in my environment who serve in the public areas such as law enforcers, teachers, medical professionals, taxi operators, ancillary workers, caretakers, garbage collectors, etc. These persons serve to ensure that I have and will continue to have a clean and safe environment, which will allow me to become a productive role model citizen for future generations.

- ✓ I am thankful for my physical and spiritual environment. My location on earth may cause me to experience or to be exposed to a variety of situations whether it be prosperity or poverty, crime, and violence, floods, hurricanes, tsunami, earthquakes, or physical, sexual, or verbal abuse. I am thankful that I will not rely on my environment to deter or distract me from my goals, but I will use this present environment as a medium to create a more exultant and sustainable environment to reside in. I am thankful for the awareness of my spirituality as I can appreciate the solar systems, the winds, rain, the elements etc. To acknowledge that there are things that I may never find the answers to that I seek butto accept or to peruse the notion that with the help of a spiritual being or beings and through thorough research and inquiry more will be learnt about planet Earth that I call home.

Create an acronym for the word THANKFUL that best defines you.

9. I am compassionate towards others.

- ✓ I am concerned about other people's thoughts, feelings, and experiences as well as my own.
- ✓ I am compassionate to other people's suffering as I am always trying to find solutions to help others alleviate their suffering. For example, if I see my classmate crying, I will try to find out what is the issue affecting him or her andthen seek assistance from others such as administrators, teachers, peers, or parents to rectify the situation.
- ✓ I will show compassion to others who I have hurt by apologizing with kindness. For example, saying words to someone that I deemed the truth, but say those words offensively, for example, if I say to my classmate "your socks are dirty and have holes in

them because you are so poor." Apologizing to the person allows the person that I have offended to see that I am showing some remorse for the previous action carried out also the person offended will feel vindicated. While I would realize that the person has no control over his or her situation and if I was in a similar or same situation, I would like someone to show compassion towards me.

- ✓ I will show compassion by forgiving those persons who havedone me wrong and are unable to acknowledge their wrongs by treating them with kindness and patience. By choosing to focus on their good attributes rather than their bad ones.

- ✓ I will be compassionate to those whom I serve and to those who are not able to care for themselves. Namely, mentally challenged persons, street persons, physically challenged persons, blind and visually impaired persons, the mute, the elderly, children, and domestic animals.

For example:
- ✓ Helping an elderly person get across a busy street.
- ✓ Volunteering in the feeding programme for the homeless during the holidays or whenever I am free to do so.

- ✓ Giving people gifts who have lost their homes because of natural disasters or fires, for example, toys, clothes, food books, devices toiletries.
- ✓ No kicking or stoning or carrying out cruel acts towards domestic or stray animals but aiding them by trying to find their owners or by gently trying to deter them from where they are to an area more suitable for them if they are causing a disturbance to you or others.
- ✓ Showing compassion also allows me to have a good inter-personal relationship with my peers and others and to be a leader who is caring to my team members and my staff members.
- ✓ It will also allow me to gain the trust and respect of my peers and others and the support of others when I may need it or in future experiences.
- ✓ Showing compassion to others will make me become a better moral and ethical leader where I can assess certain situations not only from an ethical point but also from a moral point. Even though at times it may not be easy to differentiate between morality from ethical considerations but being compassionate may allow me to have a slightly different view from that of the individual who does not practicecompassion.

- ✓ Learning to be compassionate towards others will also allow me to become self-aware that I too must practice compassion toward myself. I will become more appreciative of some of the challenges that I will face and how I will overcome them. Because of my compassion for others, I will be able to relate to the knowledge that I will make mistakes and will encounter situations in which I may not have any control over the outcomes.
- ✓ Showing compassion will add purpose to my life, by doing selfless acts I will be able to show love to others who feel unworthy of love or need love to grow in confidence.
- ✓ It will allow me to help those who may need a voice to speak for them because they are rejected by society.
- ✓ Carrying out acts of compassion will allow me to become more empathetic, altruistic, and respectful to those in my environment. Guiding me to become a charismatic and perceptive individual and a future leader who will cater to the rights of individuals and assist others who may need help.

Create an acronym for the word COMPASSIONATE that best defines you.

10. I am Respectful: respectful to authorities, my family, and respectful in my address towards others.

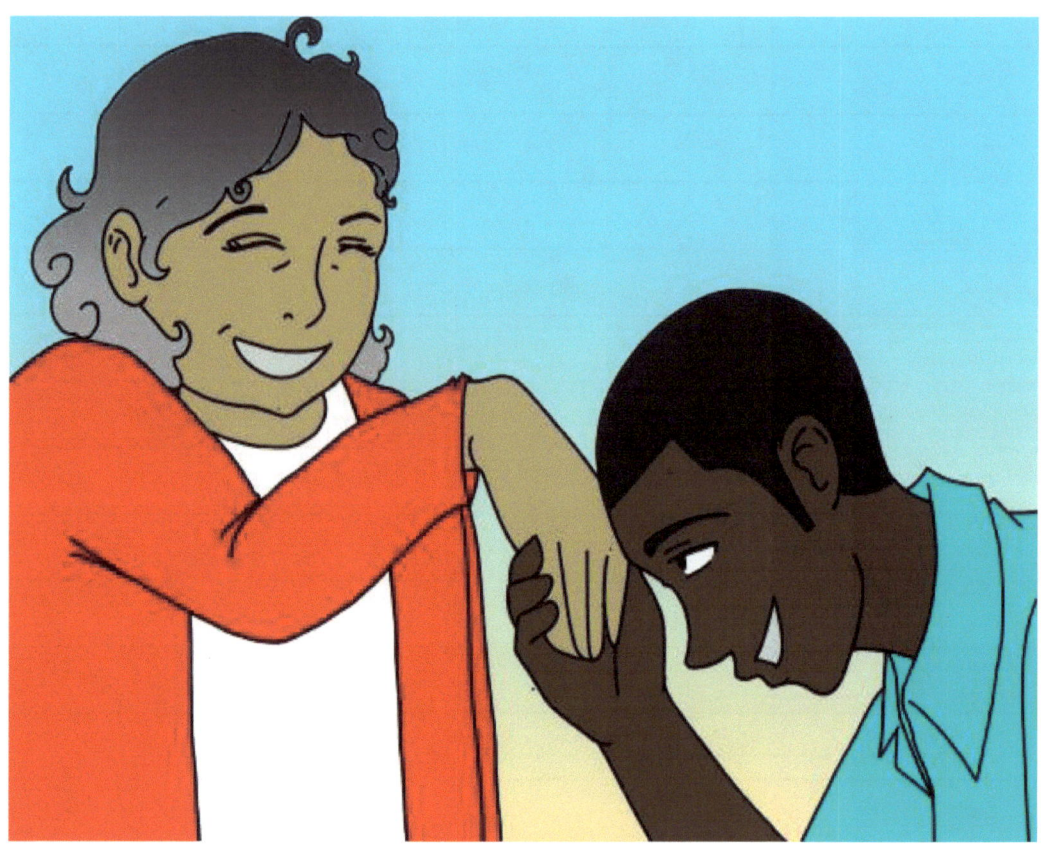

Respectful in my address to others using words such as:
- ✓ Thank you
- ✓ May I
- ✓ Excuse me
- ✓ I am sorry
- ✓ Please

Respectful in my consideration of other people's space and time

- ✓ Putting in my earbuds and earphones when listening to my videos or songs so as not to disturb others. They might not enjoy the same type of music or videos as I do. In doing this I can create a peaceful environment for others and myself. If I do not possess earbuds or earphones, I can lower the volume on my device, so I do not disturb the person sharing the space with me.
- ✓ Keeping my environment clean and tidy. Whether I share rooms with siblings or other family members I must respect other people's space. Cleaning up my mess, for example, discarding waste in the trash bags or bins, and placing dirty laundry in the laundry bin. Washing dirty plates in the sink even if it is not my chore.
- ✓ I must respect that each person has their boundary, in other words, there are some things in my environment that I am not comfortable sharing. Whether it is the wearing of my undergarments, my beauty cosmetics, my shoes, or clothes, or the reading of my diary or texts. Others sitting or lying in my bed, persons entering my house with their shoes on; therefore, if I want people to respect my space and boundaries I must also respect theirs.

I must be respectful towards another person's perspectives; not everyone will share my opinions and ideas, but I must show respect toward another person's views or perspectives. I must respect that a person has a right to freedom of speech and religion. I must acknowledge that there are multiple cultures, therefore people will have various belief and value systems. There will be some that will contradict and oppose my value system, but I must show respect to them by not:

- Bullying them
- Carrying out hate crimes toward them
- Embarrassing them
- Harassing them
- Slandering them on social media

I will show respect by trying to understand their value system through research, to achieve the appropriate knowledge. Through research I will seek the appropriate knowledge to understand their belief and value systems, I will respect the difference and their right to their value system.

Respectful in how I serve others. I must be respectful in how I help others. For example,
- ✓ Helping my younger sibling or family member to get dressed for school without complaining,
- ✓ Helping my grandma to learn a new app or by helping my neighbour with their homework with patience.
- ✓ Helping my parents wash the dishes or help to prepare a meal because I see there is a need.
- ✓ Actively listening to someone who has an issue or needs without prejudice or pride.
- ✓ Being caring and kind to those in my environment especially those that are not able to take care of themselves in such cases as the elderly, mentally challenged, and the sick.

Respecting others will also allow me to gain more self-respect and prepare me to become a productive member of the global society.

Create an acronym for the word RESPECTFUL that best defines you.

Word Search

```
X T Q Q B M T O E X O B S L B Q D E Q V S R Y Y N
H I C Q K E K C L S D A W E B K I H H D O R H L K
B K K E Q K S H O P P I N G L H R V M M X Q I L Y
Y T V S L B H M L M B D F R X F H X S J J G S I Q
T O P I O L W Z A M P N A O I F I A P L D O L P B
O K T H I C P R F K K A T N Y Z M D Z G T A Y K L
Z M D U Y W I H U W E P S C A S G E G G N L D X O
Z K H E W S S A O F D E M S I I D Z M N I O U B G
I G K T T H I E L N X E W X I E N H U T T R H X G
T V M E U E A C Z M E R D I R O A G S Y C I P Q I
W U C Z R H R T A Z E S E D X R N U I Y C E T E N
P U B E R T Y M S L F D C L V T M A C N F N P Y G
C H J D W L F J I A D R I Y A N H M T E H T R L L
H G X B T Z E M G N P E I A X T R O L E E E A V F
O J Y M R A G I J P A P V E T C I B R Y E D Y V O
R T N H E P M I S V O T Q E N R N O W M U E I T R
E A B C S P S U U U P Y I R L D I C N E O D N G G
S M Q X P S W D V R R F F O S O S L E S L N G G I
Z B C B E C D R W W I E E A N U P H F H H M E U V
G I R R C A M B I T I O U S C W R M I S E I B S E
U T M O T I V A T I O N H Z Y E U U E P Q Z P Y N
P I U R C D Y Q Z H B Y X T X H B E D N O N M S E
X O P D W T H I F L A R A G K G Q O I X T M F R S
B N I L J N O P Q O M W G H P F D R O H F K A L S
T E X T I N G U G R O W T H S P U R T K V O M C C
```

CLUES

Growth Spurt   Self-Identity   Blogging   Facebook
WhatsApp Physical Development Music Dancing Goal oriented
Shopping Compassionate   Hormones   Respect   Ambitious
Cell phone   Social Media   Leisure TikTok Friendship
Motivation   Puberty   Apps Praying   Peers Relationships
Texting Determination Praying Chores

BEING A TEENAGER ROCKS

CLUES

Across

1. Chemical substances that act like messenger molecules in the body. (8)

3. Compliance with an order, request, or law or submission to another's authority. (9)

4. The power or right to give orders, make decisions, and enforce obedience. (9)

7. Comprehensive knowledge or skill in a particular subject or activity. (7)

9. The period during which adolescents reach sexual maturity and become capable of reproduction. (7)

10. A period when a child's height rapidly increases. (6-5)

13. Conscious knowledge of one's own character and feelings. (4-9)

14. Behaviour modifications or habit changes that encourage positive changes. (9-7)

17. A standards-based sequence of planned experiences where students practice and achieve proficiency in content and applied learning skills. (10)

18. The perception or recognition of one's characteristics as a particular individual, especially in relation to social context. (4-8)

19. The ability to think about or plan the future with imaginationor wisdom. (7)

20. An event or occurrence which leaves an impression on someone. (10)

22. A person or action) creating or controlling a situation rather than just responding to it after it has happened. (9)

Down

2. The accomplishment of an aim or purpose. (6)

5. A sequence of actions regularly followed. (8)

6. The years of a person's age from 13 to 19. (4)

8. The ability to think clearly and rationally, understanding the logical connection between ideas. (8-8)

11. The ability to continue trying to do something, even if it is Difficult. (13)

12. The way in which two or more people or groups regard and behave towards each other. (12)

15. An act of choosing between two or more possibilities. (7)

16. A person or animal able to withstand or recover quickly from difficult conditions. (9)

21. An occupation undertaken for a significant period of a person's life and with opportunities for progress. (6)

www.ingramcontent.com/pod-product-compliance
Lightning Source LLC
Chambersburg PA
CBHW042023150426
43198CB00002B/52